Dealing with a Narcissist

Disarming and becoming the narcissist's
nightmare. Understanding Narcissism
& Narcissistic personality disorder.
Healing after hidden psychological and
emotional abuse

By Dr.Theresa J. Covert

Table of Contents

Introduction to Narcissism ----------------------- 4

Chapter 1: Understanding the Mind of a
Narcissist -- 7

Chapter 2: Identify the Type of Narcissist
You Are Dealing With --------------------------- 13

The Know-It-Alls -- 14

The Grandiose Narcissists ------------------------ 15

The Seducers -- 16

The Bullies -- 17

The Vindictive Narcissist ----------------------- 18

Chapter 3: Create Boundaries with the
Narcissist and Stick to the Boundaries ---- 20

Chapter 4: Empathic Validation ---------------- 25

Chapter 5: Avoid Sharing TMI (Too Much
Information) --- 30

Chapter 6: Don't Assume the Narcissist
Cares About You ------------------------------------ 35

Chapter 7: Don't Engage the Narcissist in
Psychological Games ------------------------------ 39

Chapter 8: Don't Second-Guess Your
Decisions When Dealing With a
Narcissist -- 44

Chapter 9: Try Not to Take the
Narcissist's Actions Personally --------------- 49

Chapter 10: Verify Any and All Claims
That the Narcissist Makes -------------------- 53

Chapter 11: Don't Compete With the
Narcissist --- 58
Chapter 12: Get Away From the
Narcissist --- 62
Chapter 13: Ignore the Narcissist ------------- 66
Chapter 14: 10 Things a Narcissist Will
Always Do In a Relationship------------------ 71
He Will Try to Charm You---------------------- 72
He Will Make You Feel Worthless ------------ 72
He Will Hog Your Conversations -------------- 73
He Will Violate Your Boundaries ------------- 74
He Will Break the Rules-------------------------- 74
He Will Try to Change You ---------------------- 75
He Will Exhibit a Sense of Entitlement ----- 75
He Will Try to Isolate You ---------------------- 76
He Will Express a Lot of Negative
Emotions -- 77
He Will Play the Blame Game----------------- 77
Conclusion -- 79

Introduction to Narcissism

Congratulations on downloading *Dealing with a Narcissist* and thank you for doing so.

The following chapters will discuss various tips and tricks that can help you deal with narcissistic people in your personal life and your career, but before we go into that, let's briefly introduce the concept of narcissism.

The term "narcissist' can be used to describe a fairly wide range of people. Narcissism could be manifested in a mild form in a leader who is charming and charismatic, but also a bit egotistical. On the other end of the spectrum, it could be manifested in a person with a "narcissistic personality disorder." Such a person would be grandiose to the extent that he/she gets violently angry if you don't give him/her attention or admiration.

The fact is that narcissism exists on a spectrum and even the nicest people tend to have mild narcissistic tendencies. For this book, we will be discussing how to deal with the sort of people in whom narcissism is manifested as a major personality trait.

We mistakenly attach the "narcissist" label on people who have high self-esteem, or people who talk with great pride about their careers or their personal lives. Such people aren't necessarily narcissists in the clinical sense of the word.

Narcissistic people are those who feel that they are special (more than anyone else around them), that they deserve a lot of appreciation just for giving us the time of day, but most significantly, they have a diminished sense of empathy towards others. Narcissists also have lots of other negative attributes that branch out from these main ones, and those attributes make them incapable of fulfilling other people's needs in relationships.

Narcissists aren't oblivious of the fact that they are self-centered. They are consciously aware of their selfishness, but they truly believe that the selfishness is warranted because after all, they think they are special.

Narcissists expect people to give them special treatment, so they actively manipulate and control people to ensure that they satisfy that need. Therein lays the problem for most people. If you have narcissists in your life, you can rest assured that they will try to get you to give them special treatment, because they just can't help it.

If you want to avoid ending up under the thumb of a narcissist, then reading this book is a great first step for you.

There are plenty of books on this subject on the market, thanks again for choosing this one! Every effort was made to ensure it is full of as much useful information as possible; please enjoy!

Chapter 1: Understanding the Mind of a Narcissist

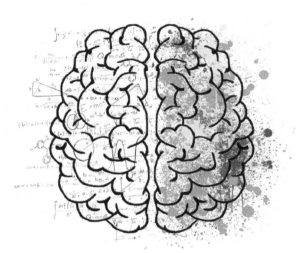

There is a common misconception that narcissists are people who love themselves a lot. In actual sense, they are people who love the way other people perceive them, and some of them actually dislike or even loathe themselves. The terms 'narcissism' and 'narcissist' come from the name 'Narcissus.' Narcissus is a character in Greek Mythology. He was a handsome hunter who was cursed by the gods to live without human love, and in the end, he could only fall in love with a reflection of himself. Like the original Narcissus, people with narcissistic personality traits don't fall in love with other people, but they instead fall in love with versions of themselves that you mirror back to them.

Narcissists are known for self-flattery. They often brag about everything, and they are insistent on making themselves seem superior to everyone else around them. That doesn't necessarily mean that they love who they are, or that they are striving for perfection in order to better themselves. More often than not, the vocal self-assuredness and the arrogance is usually a cover for a deep self-hatred that they aren't willing to open up about.

Some narcissists aren't even willing to admit their self-loathing to themselves, so they live under the delusion that they are better than everyone else and that they are immune to the shortcomings that everyone else suffers from, or that they are above almost everything. To most of them, arrogance is, in fact, a way to cope with their own shortcomings.

Narcissists tend to treat others with a lot of disdain, but that disdain is meant to conceal jealousy. If someone else is the center of attention, you can be sure that the narcissist will try to one-up him/her, and if that is not possible, the narcissist will try to criticize the person or diminish the accomplishment in one way or the other.

Narcissists often look outwards in their criticism of others, but they are very afraid to look inward to examine their own talents and attributes. Deep within, narcissists know that the truth about their own condition is quite devastating. They will make claims about how good they are at something, or how better they are than other people, but they will do everything necessary to prevent you from examining their claims too closely.

From an emotional standpoint, narcissists are dead inside. There is an emotional emptiness in them, and they are often looking to fill that emptiness with external validation. If you are around a narcissist or you are in a relationship with one, all they are going to do is seek constant validation from you. When they lie to make they seem smarter or more accomplished, it's in service of seeking respect and validation from you. If they keep trying to manipulate you emotionally, it's because they want to control the way you perceive them for the purposes of validation. If they react angrily or violently in certain situations, it's because they feel like they are not getting the validation they were hoping to get from you at that point in time.

The irony is that although narcissists are always looking for validation, they can never give it to other people. You know that human relationships are based on reciprocity, so if you give validation to someone, they are more likely to give it back to you. Narcissists want you to validate them, but they will never validate you (unless they are trying to manipulate you). Narcissists are incapable of appreciating love, so if you express love (or any other positive emotion) towards them, they will either alienate you or they will trample all over that love.

To fully understand the narcissistic mind, let's look at the diagnostic criteria that are used by mental health professionals and psychologists to identify them. Here are the nine main characteristics of narcissists:

1. They feel a high level of self-importance, and they often exaggerate their capabilities and their accomplishments.

2. They dream of having unlimited control, power, attractiveness, intelligence, and success.

3. They think they are special and one-of-a-kind and they want to be associated with high-class people or entities.

4. They are always looking to be excessively admired.

5. They are always looking for special treatment, and they always expect you to comply with their wishes or demands.

6. They won't hesitate to take advantage of your for their own personal gains.

7. They don't empathize with others. It's always about them, so they won't go out of their way to accommodate your needs.

8. They are always jealous of others, and they wrongly believe that others are jealous of them.

9. They are very arrogant, in both their
   words and their actions.

Now, we all may have one or more of these
traits in us, but narcissists are those who tend
to have most of these traits and to exhibit them
constantly.

Chapter 2: Identify the Type of Narcissist You Are Dealing With

Narcissism manifests itself in many different ways, so there are many types of narcissists. You can categorize narcissists according to the way they act in relationships, or according to the traits that they manifest more often. In this chapter, we will look at the five main types of narcissists. If you spend a lot of time with a narcissistic person, you may find that they show signs that fall under more than one of the categories we will discuss in this chapter, but when you want to figure out which category a particular narcissist falls under, always go with the one that covers his/her most dominant traits. Here are the five main types of narcissists that you are likely to deal with at some point in your life:

The Know-It-Alls

These are narcissists who believe that they are always the "smartest guy in the room," and they are very concerned with making sure that everyone knows it. They will give their opinion even when no one asked for it. They will insist on being the center of the conversation, even if the topic under discussion is clearly not in their area of expertise. They will often give you advice that seems helpful in their minds but is of no actual value to you.

These narcissists also make for terrible listeners because, when it's your turn to speak during the conversation, instead of paying attention to what you are saying, they are always thinking about what to say next. They are always ready and willing to offer you long lectures, just to let you know how much they know, and they have a difficult time letting anyone else speak.

The Grandiose Narcissists

These are the kind of narcissists that always wants to appear more important and more influential than anyone else. They never shut up about their accomplishments, and they are always trying to convince people that they are more successful than they actually are. They are always looking to gain the envy and the admiration of others.

These narcissists always believe that they are destined for greater things than anyone else around, and they may act in a selfish way because they believe their special status entitles them to preferential treatment. In fact, they think that if they receive preferential treatment, it is in service of some kind of social good. They believe that they belong at the top of the pyramid of some sort of social hierarchy, whether it's at work, or at home.

One interesting thing about grandiose narcissists is that sometimes, their grandiosity can be a self-fulfilling prophecy. Some of them are more driven, and also a bit charismatic as a result of their grandiosity. In the end, that causes them to succeed. Sometimes, people may start to revere them, and they may put them in positions of power.

The Seducers

These are narcissists who tend to manipulate people for their own benefit. Unlike other narcissists, these ones may actually make you feel good about yourself, but that feeling never actually lasts — it ends as soon as they get what they want.

Seducers will start off by expressing admiration for you, but it's always just something that they think you want to hear, and the point is to get you to offer them the same admiration so that they can take advantage of you.

Once the seducers have gotten what they want from you, they reveal their true colors, and they pull the rug from under your feet. Such a person may keep offering you compliments, but the moment you comply with their request, they start giving you the cold shoulder.

If you are dealing with a person who keeps flattering you, try to see if he/she does the same with everyone else. If the niceness is only directed towards you, the reason could be that they are targeting you for manipulation.

The Bullies

These narcissists work under the assumption that one builds himself or herself up by tearing down or humiliating others. The purpose of bullying is to assert one's superiority, and this kind of narcissist is really brutal in the way he/she does this. We are not talking here about the school-yard bully – the narcissistic bully is a lot more sophisticated than that (although his/her methods may be somewhat similar to the ones of the school-yard bully).

This kind of narcissist treats others with contempt, in the hope that they will feel like losers, allowing him/her to feel like a winner in the process. This is the kind of person that will disparage you at every turn, and he will undermine and pour cold water on all your efforts at self-improvement. Their criticism is never constructive — it is meant to mock you and tell you that you are not capable or worthy of improvement. When this type of narcissist wants something from you, he/she doesn't ask for it, he/she demands it; as though it's something you owe him/her.

The Vindictive Narcissist

This is the kind of narcissist that is out to destroy you. This narcissist is destructive by nature, and to him/her, everything and everyone that challenges their superiority have to be brought down.

These narcissists tend to target people for reasons that the average person would consider mundane. They hold grudges that are completely one-sided. These are the kinds of people who think of you as their ultimate nemesis just because you stepped on their toes by accident a few months ago.

The vindictive narcissist can't let anything go, no matter whom silly it may seem to you. If it's someone in your social circle, he/she could trash-talk you to your friends or family (in your absence) just to make you look bad. If it's a colleague, they may make up stuff about you in an attempt to get you fired. If it's a former spouse, he/she can try to turn your kids against you. They may pose as victims to make you look like some sort of predator, or to make you look "crazy."

Chapter 3: Create Boundaries with the Narcissist and Stick to the Boundaries

You have to know where to draw the line with the narcissistic person. You have to decide beforehand what sort of behavior you are willing to put up with, but you also need to have strict rules for yourself about the things that you aren't willing to tolerate. Don't just go in with vague mental boundaries. In fact, wherever you can, you should create clear, well-defined boundaries, write them down, and do everything in your power to enforce them. Unless you have clear boundaries, a narcissist will walk all over you, and you will be stuck making excuses for his/her behavior.

One area where we have difficulty setting boundaries with narcissists is in the amount of time and attention that we give to them. In our minds, we always feel the need to stick around and keep interacting with anyone who tries to talk to us. It's like they have this strange ability to hold us hostage. That means that you have to make a conscious effort to resist the urge to be complacent when a narcissist hogs your time. If for instance a narcissist keeps talking on the phone when you have important things to do, just say you have to go and hang up before he has the opportunity to talk you out of it. As we've mentioned, they demand a lot of attention, and unless you set limits, they won't stop.

When you set a boundary with a narcissist, you can rest assured that they are going to test that boundary, and they are going to push it as far as you will let them. So, you have to go in with the conviction that your boundaries are not up for discussion. For example, the narcissist who keeps hogging up your time will try out all kinds of tricks to keep you talking to them, to see if you are flexible on the boundary that you have set.

For the narcissist, it's all about control, so he/she will do everything imaginable to regain control over you once you've set the boundary. He may try to convince you that you are unfair to him by denying him attention. He may try to argue with you, intimidate you, guilt you, or even confuse you. If you show any kind of flexibility, he will keep pushing at it until he knocks down your boundary. It may seem rude on your part, but if the narcissist insists on talking to you on the phone when you have made it clear that you don't have the time, just say bye and hang up.

When you set your boundary, don't explain yourself more than once. Let's take the example of a narcissist that keeps insulting you during an interaction. In this case, you will set a boundary by telling him that if he keeps being disrespectful, you are going to walk away. Of course, he is going to test you by insulting you again. Once he does this, put your money where your mouth is and walk away.

If you explain yourself a second time, that is a concession, and it will have a domino effect, and the end result will be detrimental to your stance. A narcissist will violate your boundaries intentionally, and he will always have a ready excuse to explain why that violation was warranted. If you tell him not to call you late at night, he will call, and he will pretend that he totally forget about your warning. So, when the phone rings despite your warning, ignore it. If someone pretends not to remember something you explicitly asked them not to do, they are manipulating you.

You have to remember that you don't have to explain yourself or to justify your actions to anyone. They are not the boss of you, and they don't get to interrogate you on matters that are personal to you. If you feel like saying "No" to someone over anything, it's entirely up to you to decide if you want to explain it to them (unless it's your boss at work, and even then, there are limitations to that). You have to understand that any information you offer to a narcissist will be used against you in that interaction (or in future interactions).

Narcissists always believe that they are more important than you, so to them, your boundaries are always up for review. So, you have to remember that setting and enforcing boundaries with narcissists isn't a one-time event. If it's someone that is in your life, you have to stay vigilant and to enforce your boundaries consistently. For example, if you ask a narcissist to stop hogging your time, he may stop temporarily, but a few days later, he will start testing the waters to see if you have loosened your stance. When you set your boundaries, be mentally prepared to deal with the fact that the narcissist will keep trying to abolish them for as long as you keep associating with him/her.

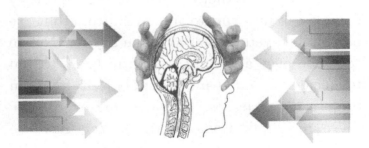

Chapter 4: Empathic Validation

When dealing with a narcissist, you have to be very careful about how you criticize his/her behavior or actions. Narcissists don't deal well with criticism. Although they are great at dishing it out, they are extremely thin-skinned when they are the ones being criticized, and they may lash out in ways that could harm you a lot more. So, to be able to criticize a narcissist effectively, you should learn to use emphatic validation.

Emphatic validation is a technique used to deliver criticism by concealing it in the midst of

25

compliments. Most people are receptive of critical notions about them if the criticism is sandwiched between 2 compliments.

We have mentioned that narcissists live for validation, so if you want to criticize one, you have to make sure that the criticism is disguised as validation. It's not that we don't want you to value brutal honesty here; it's just that we are trying to get you to be more tactful in your approach. Brutal honesty will only serve to aggravate the narcissist, and it will put you in his/her crosshairs, so it will be to your own detriment. Avoid brutal honesty, but try to be as sincere as possible.

So, as you approach a narcissist in an attempt to critique him/her, think long and hard about the structure of the conversation that is about to ensue. Have some sort of outline in your head before you start to speak. Preparation is the key, and you have to be able to anticipate and respond appropriately to some of the reactions that he/she may have. Walk through the conversation in your head try as much as possible to use positive language. You have to express yourself calmly and firmly because narcissists only respond to strength and not to weakness.

Come up with positive compliments with which to start your conversations. You can play into the narcissist's believes about himself or herself. If it's someone close to you, it's likely that you already know what it is that he/she wants to hear, so it wouldn't be too difficult to come up with compliments that they will respond to.

Your compliments can include a wide range of observations that you have made about the person lately, but you should try to give compliments that are closely related to the criticism that you want to dish out, because you don't want the criticisms to seem out of context (if the criticism comes out of left-field, the narcissist will know that your intention was always to be critical, and he/she will definitely hold it against you).

After you are done with your opening compliment, you want to use transitional words before you toss in your constructive criticism. Here, you want to make sure that your criticism sounds like a "by the way" without making it sound too insignificant.

Next, it's time to deliver the criticism. There is an art to doing this. You want the narcissist to feel like their way of doing things is almost perfect, but it would be completely perfect if they added this one minor correction. Since narcissists aspire to be perfect, they are likely to respond to your constructive criticism because they believe it would make them seem even more perfect in your eyes than they already are.

One technique you can use here is to make it seem as though the idea was his/hers all along. Since the narcissist wants to seem smarter than you, you can suggest several solutions to a problem (of those solutions, only one should be truly viable) and then leave it to him/her to make the decision as to which solution to implement for that particular situation. Narcissists love to take credit for other people's ideas, so you can structure the constructive criticism in a way that makes it easy for them to take credit for the idea of the change for which you are advocating.

You have to finish off by adding a few compliments so that you don't leave the narcissist with feelings of inadequacy. You can also try to paint a picture of how "awesome" things will be for the narcissist if he/she decided to incorporate your criticisms into his/her life.

There are a few things to remember as you use emphatic validation with a narcissist. First, you have to make sure that you pass your message across. It's a tight rope to walk, but it is doable. Secondly, you have to be careful about when and where you deliver your constructive criticism. It's okay to deal with some topics in the presence of other people, but there are topics that you must strictly bring up in private (the higher the potential for embarrassment, they more important it is for you to do it in private).

Chapter 5: Avoid Sharing TMI (Too Much Information)

You probably already make a conscious effort to avoid revealing too much information when interacting with people at work, or even friends you don't fully trust. With narcissistic people, you have to filter your personal information even more than you are used to. Narcissists have the uncanny ability to use any kind of information against you, so don't trust them with any personal details.

You have to remember that the narcissist is going to actively seek out information about you under the guise of social discourse, but with bad intentions. They are going to pretend to be interested in you as a way to manipulate you and to elicit personal information from you. They'll do everything they can to put you at ease so that you let your guard down and spill all your secrets.

If you find that the narcissist is prying into your personal life, you have to shut it down. If they keep asking personal questions, make it clear that you have no intention of sharing that kind of information with them or with anyone else (tell them that it's not just them you don't want to talk to about your personal life and that you are just a private person). You have to make sure that it appears that you are private on general principle and that you are not just keeping information from the narcissist because you don't trust him/her.

Where private information is concerned, if you have identified someone as a narcissist, you have to tell all the friends and the family member that you confide in to keep your secrets from him or her. If a narcissist is out to get you and he/she finds that you are unwilling to provide personal information, he/she could decide to manipulate the people that are close to you in order to get it from them, so make sure that you swear your friends to secrecy where he/she is concerned.

Keeping your personal information from a narcissist is easier said than done. The fact is that these days, it's very easy to gain access to someone's personal information because we willingly share more than we need to online, and a narcissist who is interested in you can discern a lot about you from your social media accounts and the people in your social circles. So, you should be extremely careful about the kind of information that you divulge on social media platforms or even to the people around you. Even if there is no narcissist in your life right now, you never know when one might show up, and you want to avoid making it easy for someone to ruin your life.

To a narcissist, information is a weapon. Narcissists have perfected the art of turning even seemingly mundane facts into serious venom. They can make up lies or exaggerate your shortcomings, and even simple facts about your life can make them seem more credible when they are spinning their lies to mutual friends and acquaintances.

Let's say a narcissist knows which street or which building you live in. If he/she is malicious and out to get you, he/she could make up anything about you, and then drop in that simple fact. For example, a malicious colleague could say he saw you buying drugs on a corner of the street you live in. Because other people in your office know you live there, his made-up story will come across as significantly more credible than it would if he hadn't tossed in that information about you.

The point is that your threshold for what you consider as personal information should be a lot lower when you are dealing with narcissists than when you are dealing with other people. In fact, avoid sharing even the most obvious information with them if you can. If they are strangers, don't give them your phone number or tell them where you live out of politeness. If they are already in your life, try as much as possible to limit the new information that you give them.

If a narcissist finds out some personal information about you, there are things you can do to make that information less potent in case he/she decides to use it against you. If you discover that someone is a narcissist after you have already told them some details about yourself, try to think back and remember what it is they know about you, and then, in the spirit of transparency, make that information known to more people so that it has no potency if the narcissist decides to use it against you. At least this way, you can control how the information comes out.

Chapter 6: Don't Assume the Narcissist Cares About You

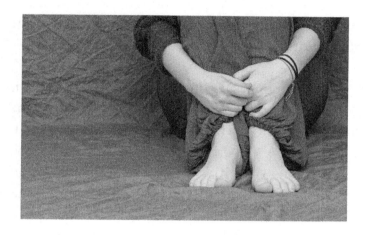

You can be forgiven for thinking that the narcissist cares about you because most humans have this innate desire to care about each other, and our default setting is to assume that others are also capable of caring about us. When you start out with the narcissist, he will give you the impression that he cares, but that is all an illusion because he wants something out of it. When the narcissist finally reveals his true colors, and you realize that he doesn't care, it can be a disconcerting experience, and you can even remain in denial about it for a very long time. That is because we are wired to look for the good in others, and when there is none to find, we keep digging deep. Don't waste your time that way — once you figure out that someone is a narcissist, it's time for the assumption that he cares to go out of the window.

If the narcissist is someone very close to you, he can start exhibiting cruel behavior that could be a major threat to you from a physical, emotional or even financial point of view. While you are still searching for the good in the person, he/she will keep taking advantage of you, and he/she will give you emotional wounds that could last a lifetime. In some cases, he/she could become physically violent. If you are a couple, he/she could also start spending all your money on things that benefit him/her without telling you, and then coming up with absurdly selfish explanations for this behavior.

Remember that the narcissist is quite devious, and he/she can take advantage of the fact that you think there is some good in him/her by feigning it once in a while to keep you on the hook. For example, if you are married to a narcissist who spends the cash in your joint accounts on things that benefit only him/her and put you in a financial quagmire, if he/she figures out that you are growing weary and you are about to leave, he/she may decide to spend some of that money on a "gift" for you, just to get you thinking again that maybe he/she isn't that bad.

An emotionally abusive narcissist may decide to buy you flowers once in a while just to get you thinking that maybe all is not lost in that relationship. You have to remember that these are just tricks that are meant to manipulate you so that you can stick around and suffer more abuse. In the narcissist's mind, he/she probably thinks that the occasional decent act negates all the horrible things that he/she does to you. Don't be fooled by the occasional kind acts.

You might ask, if a narcissist doesn't care, then why does he/she give me so much attention? This is a very confusing thing, and it has led many people to excuse the behavior of the narcissists in their lives for a long time. The truth is that for narcissists, attention is about control, having power over you, and manipulating you. Tricking you into thinking they care about you is like a sport to them, and they have a lot of fun with it. It's a sick game that they play with you to gain your trust. Once you trust them, they are going to manipulate you and bring out your insecurities so that you are somewhat dependent on them for emotional stability.

The sooner you accept the fact that the narcissist doesn't care, the sooner you will be able to get out from under his/her control, and the sooner you will be able to start healing and rebuilding your self-esteem. The longer you are stuck thinking the narcissist cares, the harder it will be for you to free yourself from his/her influence. There are people who have tolerated narcissists for so long, to the point that they have become numb to their own suffering and they have accepted the abuse as part of their existence. Don't let the narcissist break you, and don't lose perspective — you know a caring person when you see one, so don't make excuses for the narcissist.

Chapter 7: Don't Engage the Narcissist in Psychological Games

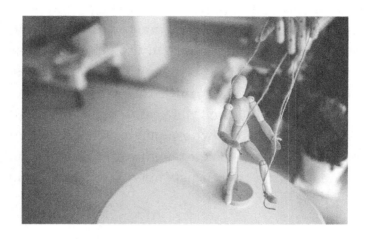

Narcissists are very good at initiating dramatic psychological games, often at your expense. They can stir up conflict between you and other people, and once you are at each other's throats, they'll pretend they had absolutely nothing to do with the situation at hand. So, if you sense that a narcissist is playing some sort of mind game with the intention of getting you to react in an aggressive way, you should take a step back.

Narcissists play games and start drama because they enjoy the chaos that ensues as a result of their machinations. When a narcissist starts a conflict between two people, he/she feels a sense of superiority over them — it feels like he/she is the puppet-master and you and others are tiny puppets ready to rip each other apart while he/she plays god over your lives. So, before you fall into the trap that the narcissist sets for you, and find yourself tangled in a drama whose origin you can't even remember, let's look at some of the common games that a narcissist may try to get you involved in.

One common game that narcissists play is the "emotional ping pong" game. This is where a person avoids taking responsibility for their actions by throwing that responsibility back to you. If the narcissist has done something reprehensible, instead of reflecting on his/her own actions and admitting wrongdoing, he/she will throw the ball back at you somehow. He/she could try to blame you, shame you, project fault onto you, or even outright deny doing something wrong, making you seem crazy for even pointing it out. If you care about him/her, you might find yourself believe the lie and even making excuses on his/her behalf.

Narcissists always love to play different variations of the 'game' where they make you seem crazy in front of other people. A narcissist could do something that indicates to you that they have malicious intent, but when you confront them, they can accuse you of having an overactive imagination, feigning innocence, or they can turn it around by accusing you of malice.

They could even get everyone around you to turn against you by making outrageous public accusations. Once you fall into that trap, you will start spinning out of control trying to prove to others that you are right, but that will only serve to prove the narcissist right. You have to learn to avoid reacting dramatically to the actions of a narcissist, and you have to be able to tell when you are being set up (with a narcissist, always assume that he/she is setting you up for something).

The most infuriating game that narcissists play is "gaslighting." This is where the narcissist flatly denies remembering something that you know perfectly well happened, and they insist that their memory is perfect and that you are the one who is mistaken. This is a very dangerous game, and it is surprisingly common in abusive relationships. If you stay for long with someone who "gaslights" you, in the end, you will start doubting your own perception of reality, and you will lose trust in your own recollection of events, your own reasoning, and intuition, and you will become a sitting duck for the abusive narcissist.

You have to remember to let the narcissist's games roll off your back because if you internalize everything that the narcissist tries to do to you if you fall into every trap he sets for you, if you give in and react in a dramatic way, in the end, you will lose.

If you play the narcissist's game for a long time, ultimately, you will suffer what pop-psychologists refer to as "death by a thousand cuts." This is where the narcissist will harm you in small ways over and over again until, in the end, he/she is able to destroy you completely. If you play the narcissist's games, he will destroy every part of you, by disparaging your accomplishments, destroying your ego and your confidence, casting doubt on your values and your belief system, and dampening your soul. If you let a narcissist have his/her way, he/she will turn everything that you are doing into a failure. If you are in a relationship, he/she will assign you the blame for everything that goes wrong, and take credit for everything that goes right.

Don't engage in the narcissist's drama. Don't play games. As a decent person, you will be inhibited by your rationality and your sense of decency. The narcissist won't play by any rules, so you can be absolutely certain that you will lose. The best way to win with a narcissist is to avoid playing his/her games altogether.

Chapter 8: Don't Second-Guess Your Decisions When Dealing With a Narcissist

You don't need to justify yourself to the narcissist. When you interact with a narcissist, he/she will insist that you explain certain actions and choices that you have taken. You have to remember that your decisions are in your own best interests, and you don't owe the narcissist any explanation. Once you bother to explain yourself to the narcissist, it opens the door for him/her to then plant the seed of doubt on the decision that you have made with the intention of making you second guess yourself so that they can regain control over you. By all means, don't explain yourself. Let them know that you have already made a decision and that you are not seeking their input on the matter. It may seem rude, but it's necessary.

You can be certain that the narcissists will keep pushing for you to explain things to them. As we have mentioned in the last chapter, the only way to win a narcissist's game is to avoid playing it altogether. The narcissist will go out of his/her way to make you think that they are just trying to help, or that they are just making friendly conversation, but once you take the bait and offer an explanation for an action you have taken or a decision you have made, the narcissist will come up with a hundred different questions and observations, all of which are tailor-made to diminish your conviction. He/she will tell you it's not in your best interest to do what you are doing, you are not smart enough or strong enough to do it, or you need their help to see your plan through.

The narcissist knows that when you start doubting your perceptions and your convictions, you will have to rely on his/her guidance a lot more and that will give him/her control over you. When you get to the point where you don't trust your own judgment, then you will accept the narcissist's judgment, and he/she will be able to tell you what to do, and how to think and act at all times.

We have mentioned gas lighting in the previous chapter, but here, we will point out some of the signs that can indicate to you that you are being gaslighted, so that you are in a better position to stop doubting yourself and to avoid further manipulation.

First, the narcissist will start by telling a blatant lie. Since this is a person that you have known for a while and you trust to some level, the lie will throw you off balance, and you will start doubting things that are obvious. Next, the narcissist will deny things that they said, even if you can prove that they did. The more vehement their denial, the more you question your own reality!

The narcissist succeeds in gas lighting you because he/she wears you down over time. It's easy to think that you are too smart to get gaslighted, but the fact is that it doesn't happen instantaneously, it happens gradually, and one day you will wake up and find that you are so far gone. The way it works is that the narcissist will tell a small lie, stick with it and make you question your reality a little bit, but then you will decide that it's too small a lie to matter, so you will let it slide. The lies will then escalate both in magnitude and in frequency, and since you let the first one slide, you will have an easy time doing the same with the subsequent lies, until you get to the point where it's a norm. So, you shouldn't second guess yourself or let an obvious lie slide for even a second. Don't let the narcissist desensitize you to his/her lies.

Narcissists have perfected the art of turning things around to make it sound like you were the selfish one when it's clear that they are taking advantage of you. While you are still confused trying to decipher what it is that they are doing, they will make great strides towards altering your whole reality.

They will also send confusing signals by occasionally acknowledging some of your claims so that you begin to think that perhaps you were mistaken about the rest of the claims. For example, if you accuse the narcissist of 3 different things, he/she could cap to one and then deny the other 2, and this makes you think that he/she might be credible to some extent.

While gas lighting and other forms of manipulation can be infuriating and confusing, they are surprisingly easy to fall for, so you have to be vigilant. Your best bet is to stick to your guns and hold on to your reality. Don't let anyone talk you out of decisions that you have made, and by all means, don't ever substitute your perception for someone else's.

Chapter 9: Try Not to Take the Narcissist's Actions Personally

To the narcissist, it's never actually about you. To him or her, you are a pawn in a mind game that they are playing, and if you weren't there, they would be doing the exact same thing to someone else. Of course, this doesn't make their abuse less painful, but at least, it clarifies things for you. It means that your suffering isn't a result of any wrongdoing on your part.

When your relationship or your association with a narcissist finally goes south (as it is bound to do) you are going to start wondering how this person that you have known and trusted could have morphed into an entirely different and mean a person who you don't recognize at all. You will start thinking that maybe you did something to deserve their anger and their animosity. In your mind, you will feel that there has to be a rational explanation for what has happened. There is, of course, a psychological explanation for the things that are happening — but you can rest assured that you didn't play a part in making those things happen. They were just meant to happen, and they were never truly within your control.

The narcissist isn't hurting you or targeting you for a personal reason. You have nothing to do with it. The narcissist acts the way he/she does because that is the nature of the beast. It may seem callous, but it's true. The narcissist targeted you because you just happened to cross his/her path, or you just happened to be in their life.

If you have a narcissistic parent, you will realize that he/she treats both you and your siblings with the same level of narcissism (it may vary at different times, but everyone gets their share of abuse over the years). If you are in a relationship with a narcissist, you can be certain that he/she treated his/her former lovers the same way. In other words, the narcissist is an equal opportunity torturer.

This information doesn't make the suffering that you endured under the narcissist any less painful, but it has several important implications for you. First, it means that there is nothing wrong with you and that there is nothing that you did to deserve what the narcissist has done to you. Many people take the abuse of narcissists because they get accustomed to the suffering, and they start internalizing the idea that they might have done something to set off the abuse (most narcissists will try to blame you for lots of things, so if you let them, they can easily convince you that you have done something to deserve the suffering).

The second implication here is that there is absolutely nothing that you could have done to control the actions of the narcissists because those are his/her natural tendencies. Many people stay in abusive relationships with narcissists because they harbor the false belief that they can change them. Now that you know the narcissist's actions aren't personal, you understand that there is no way you can control those actions, so it's futile to believe that you can change a narcissist. That should clear your conscience and make it easy for you to end the relationship or the association with the narcissist (if you can).

The third implication is that the failure of your relationship with a narcissist isn't a commentary on your ability to give or receive love (the relationship was doomed to fail from the very beginning). So, as you leave, and as you move on, you shouldn't carry the baggage from that relationship onto the next one. The only thing you should bring along with you is your newfound ability to spot a narcissist from a mile away.

Don't delude yourself into thinking that the narcissist actually cares about you because what's happening is completely and utterly impersonal. We have mentioned that some narcissists are seducers, and they can make you feel like you are the center of the universe when they are looking to manipulate you. When this happens, it can be very tempting to ignore your instincts and everything you have learned so far about narcissists, but you have to stay strong and retain your rationality.

Chapter 10: Verify Any and All Claims That the Narcissist Makes

Narcissists are natural experts at lying. That is because they have learned to rationalize their lying, and they no longer feel any guilt the way ordinary people do when they mislead others. The next time the narcissist makes an outrageous claim, especially if it's about a mutual friend, take time to investigate the claim. Trust your own judgment about the person that the narcissist is making accusations against.

The most hardened narcissists could even pass polygraph tests while telling blatant lies because they are so adept at lying, that there is no cognitive dissonance that could cause a spike in their vitals. Some psychologists have come up with the hypothesis that narcissists lie about 80 to 90 percent of the time, and they even lie about petty and inconsequential things. Narcissists will only tell the truth when it benefits them.

To be safe, you have to treat every story you hear from the narcissist with a lot of skepticism. You have to start with the assumption that everything is a lie until you prove otherwise. As you do your realities check, here are some things that you need to pay attention to in order to figure out what the actual facts are and what the narcissist is lying about:

If the narcissist casts him/herself as some kind of hero in the story, you can rest assured that you are being lied to. We have already discussed how the narcissist has an overinflated ego, so as he/she creates a fictional story to manipulate you, he/she won't be able to resist the urge to be the hero in the story. If a narcissist tells you that a friend of yours was talking ill about you, he/she will claim to have been your only advocate in that conversation.

In an attempt to seem heroic and superior, the narcissist will also come up with stories about meeting (or being friends) with famous people, going to exotic places, or being an instrumental part of some groundbreaking accomplishment that you may be vaguely familiar with. These stories are often unprompted or out of topic, but the narcissist will bend over backward to make them seem relevant to the conversation that you are having.

As they try to manipulate you, one thing many narcissists tend to do is try to make themselves your best friend, so if the narcissist accuses a friend you have known for years of things that are clearly out of character, you should know that not only is he/she lying to you, it's likely that he/she is also telling similar lies about you to your friend in order to drive a wedge between the two of you.

In many cases, narcissists will also spin stories to cast themselves as victims even though they are the actual perpetrators. When a narcissist gets in trouble with a third party, he/she will come to you telling stories about being wronged, being treated unfairly, and how he/she went out of the way to be the bigger person. Even if you were there and you witnessed the whole thing, you will find the narcissist trying to convince you that things didn't go down as you thought and that you were the one who didn't pay enough attention.

If you catch a narcissist doing something wrong, he/she may also try to get out of the situation by spinning a story about how he/she was messed up as a child or in a past relationship and that his/her bad behavior is a consequence of past traumatic events. The narcissist may try to get you to empathize with him/her by saying how he/she has been working on this one weakness and how you shouldn't give up on him/her. This kind of lie often works in a relationship in which you already feel invested. That kind of "confession" can make anyone seem endearing.

If a narcissist tells you that he is coming from a dark place, he is sorry, and he is on a journey to change his life, you should be greatly alarmed. If you let the narcissist off the hook because of a story like that, he is going to use the same story over and over again, and the more times you let it go, the harder it would be for you to take a different stance in the future.

When narcissists spin a story, they are going to inject a few half-truths into that story to make it seem more credible to you. You should be keen to note if the narcissist adds "facts" into the story, including places you are familiar with, days you vaguely recall, or people you used to know. The intention is to make you more inclined to believe him/her. You should pay attention to the unnecessary details that the narcissist throws into the story, and the detail he/she brings to your attention with a bit of emphasis, then if you can, fact-check those details. More often than not, they are all lies.

Chapter 11: Don't Compete With the Narcissist

You don't want to put yourself on the spot when you are dealing with a narcissist, so the worst possible thing that you can do is try to compete with him/her on trivial things that don't actually matter to you. Narcissists take trivial competitions seriously, and if you try to one-up them in any way, you will end up losing.

There is one simple reason why you are going to lose. The narcissist is ready and willing to cross lines that you as a reasonable person will never dream of crossing. You don't operate under the same rules of decency, so if you try to one-up a narcissist, your own conscience will keep you from winning.

Another important thing to note is that even if you one-up a narcissist and you win by all objective standards, the narcissist will just declare himself the winner anyway and there is absolutely nothing you can do about it. Victory against a narcissist will never be as sweet as you hoped because he will never acknowledge it or give you any respect as a result of your victory. He will just tell people the opposite thing happened, and you will then seem petty if you try to insist that you were victorious.

When dealing with a narcissist, your first instinct should be self-preservation and trying to one-up the narcissist won't help you with that. If you try to compete with a narcissist, you are only going to make yourself more of a target, and that could lead to your destruction. We are not suggesting that you be submissive and let the narcissist walk all over you, we are saying that you should be above it, and you should avoid getting down and dirty with the narcissist. Narcissists want to feel like they are winning over you, but if you don't try to one-up them, you are essentially telling them that you don't care about their silly games, and this may make them go out and try to find someone else over whom to assert their dominance.

If you avoid one-upping a narcissist, he could stop bothering you because it's just not fun for him. For example, if a narcissistic colleague starts telling you how smart and knowledgeable he is, you can just say "good for you" and carry on with your work. Because he wants to feel in control, the fact that you seem calm and unfettered will tell him that he may be out of his depth here, and he could proceed to find someone else to bug in order to feel superior. However, if you respond to his assertions by telling him where you went to school and how much experience you have, he will take that as a challenge, and he will never seize trying to prove he is smarter than you.

Once you try to one-up a narcissist, you are in a game that is going to last for the remainder of your relationship or your association with the narcissist. The only way that game is going to end is if you admit defeat, so the best thing for you is to never get into it in the first place.

When we one-up people in normal social situations, it's because we want them to think highly of us, but the thing with narcissists is that no matter how accomplished we are, they are never going to think highly of us or to give us the respect we deserve. So, if you really think about it, there is no upside to one-upping a narcissist. Only misery can come out of the decision to do such a thing.

It's possible to one-up a narcissist unintentionally, without ever realizing it, and when this happens, the consequences can be disastrous. There are things that you can do avoid inadvertently one-upping a narcissist. For example, when you are talking to other people about things that you have accomplished recently, you can avoid using the word "I" and instead use the word "we" so that the narcissist doesn't feel slighted. If the narcissist is a colleague with whom you have worked on a project, when you report to your boss in his presence, don't say "I solved the issue," instead, say "we solved the issue." The narcissist likes to hog credit, but he would rather share it with you than not get it at all.

Chapter 12: Get Away From the Narcissist

You have to get away from the narcissist because staying is not good for you in the long-run. However, there are situations where the narcissist in question is a vital part of your life, and it's utterly impractical for you to leave him/her completely. For instance, he/she could be a spouse with whom you have kids, a family member, or a colleague in your department. In such cases, you can try to put as much distance between the two of you as possible while at the same time trying to limit the harm that befalls your kids, your other family members or your career respectively.

If your lives aren't already intertwined, you can break up with them, leave them, and avoid contacting them altogether. Remember that they didn't really care about you, so don't worry too much about how they are going to feel after you break up.

Don't bother explaining too much detail about why you are leaving. Remember that if you take the time to justify yourself, they are going to try to talk you out of it. Break up in a public place and leave, never to return. Don't agree to be friends with them or to hang out in the future, no matter how insistent they are.

Some psychologists even suggest that you should break up with narcissists over the phone because there is no way of telling how in-person meetings are going to go. When you avoid contact with the narcissist, tell him that he is not welcome into your home, and block his number from your phone. If you leave the tiniest window open, he is going to find a way to crawl back into your life. Don't do any lingering goodbye. Just say your piece and leave.

There are always going to be some mutual friends who are going to vouch for the narcissist and tell you that you made a mistake leaving him. These friends may mean well, but they certainly don't fully understand how much you have been suffering under the thumb of the narcissist. With them, you have to make it clear that the narcissist is persona non grata, and the cost of bringing him up during your conversations is that they will lose your friendship. Tell them that you don't want any updates on the narcissist's life, and if they still talk to him, they shouldn't tell him anything about you either.

When you leave a narcissist, that very same day, write down exactly why you left him. In your journal, put down the rationale for your decision, and all the reasons why being with him was a bad thing for you. The purpose of this is that when the narcissist comes crawling back into your life and tries to manipulate you, you can refer back to your journal and remember why it's vital that you stay away from him. We have talked about gas lighting and how a manipulative narcissist can get you to question your own sanity, so having contemporaneous records of your thoughts and feelings can help you stay grounded on the truth.

If you successfully get away from a narcissist, hopefully, he/she will move on quickly, find someone else torment, and leave you alone. Because the narcissist never really cared about you in the first place, he won't be too hung up on your relationship, so don't question your decision when you see that he/she has moved on too quickly and you start to worry that you may end up alone. Being alone is better than being with someone who sucks the life out of you.

Chapter 13: Ignore the Narcissist

The narcissist lives to trigger emotional reactions in people because, in their minds, that gives them some sense of power. If a narcissist causes you to lose control over your emotions, it gives him a lot of satisfaction. When a narcissist attacks you verbally, ignoring him can drive him crazy.

You have to understand that narcissists crave attention, so ignoring them hurts them more than anything else. They want to be acknowledged and validated; that is why they start with the conflict in the first place. When a narcissist targets you and destroys your life, your natural instinct will be to get back at him/her by reacting angrily and emotionally, but if you do that, you are only playing into his/her hand.

It may not seem so at first, but over time, you will realize that ignoring the narcissist is actually much more satisfying than engaging with him/her because then, even to third-party observers, the narcissist will just seem like a petty person who likes to pick fights with people, and you will seem like the mature adult who is able to rise above it all.

The narcissist wants to control you and to assert dominance over you, but you have to remember that people can't take power from you. You actually have to give it to them. A narcissist can only have dominance over you if you relinquish control to him/her. As we have mentioned, you are guaranteed to lose if you play the narcissist's game, and that is when he/she is actually capable of dominating you. By ignoring the narcissist, you blatantly refuse to play his/her game, and then he/she has no means with which to get close enough to have any form of control over your life.

In as much as ignoring the narcissist hurts him/her; remember that you are doing it for yourself and for your own peace of mind. When you choose to ignore a narcissist, don't be preoccupied with the effect that the lack of attention has on him/her. Focus on doing something worthwhile for yourself. If after ignoring the narcissist, you are still obsessed with how he/she is reacting to it, then you are still under his/her control, and you are relinquishing your power to him/her.

When you ignore an ex who is a narcissist, don't turn around and start stalking him on social media to see if he is miserable. Now that you have regained control, you should focus on detoxifying from the narcissist's influence and training yourself to be more vigilant in the future.

If the narcissist is someone who is in your life permanently, ignoring him/her is going to be a regular thing, so you have to train yourself so as to get better at it. Ignoring a narcissist is more than just avoiding responding to their taunts. It's about learning to stop caring about their opinions and their criticisms. The first step is to restrain yourself from responding to them even if their comments hurt you, but after that, you have to work on yourself to get to the point where what they say rolls off you like water.

Remember that although you have no control over what the narcissist says, you have control over how much importance you associate with the things he/she says or does. Once you figure out that a person is a narcissist, you should make a conscious effort to stop attaching any actual meaning or value to their words and actions. Just regard them as malicious, and assume all their actions towards you are ill-conceived. That way, you are less likely to get hurt by them.

When you ignore a narcissist, you have to keep your safety in mind. Some narcissists tend to turn aggressive or violent when you deny them attention, so you have to be careful not to be anywhere with them without witnesses present. Ignoring a narcissist makes him/her feel that you have slipped away from his/her control, and in a desperate effort to regain that control, you never know how they are going to lash out. You have to be a lot more cautious and a lot smarter going forward because the narcissist is going to bring his/her "A" game in order to regain control over you. Keep ignoring them, and no matter how hard they come at you, don't relent, not even slightly.

Chapter 14: 10 Things a Narcissist Will Always Do In a Relationship

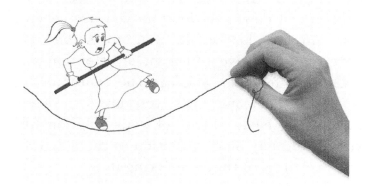

You can be able to tell if the person you are in a relationship with is a narcissist based on the kind of behavior he/she exhibits throughout the duration of your relationship. Ideally, you want to be able to figure out if your boyfriend, girlfriend, or even an acquaintance has narcissistic tendencies as soon as possible so that you can sever ties with him/her before you are too invested in that relationship. Here are ten things that a narcissist will always do in a relationship.

71

He Will Try to Charm You

As we've mentioned throughout the book, narcissists can be quite charismatic and charming when they want something from you. If you are in a relationship with one, he will go out of his way to make you feel special in the beginning so that you trust him enough to let your guard down. As long as you are serving the purpose he wants you to serve; the narcissist will give you a lot of attention and make you feel like you are the center of his world. If someone puts you on a pedestal during the early stages of your relationship, you should pay more attention to the way they act, just to see if they are faking it.

He Will Make You Feel Worthless

After you have been hanging out with a narcissist for a while, you will notice that when you have any sort of disagreement or argument, his first instinct is to dismiss you in a way that makes you feel worthless. He will criticize you in the sort of contemptuous tone that will make you feel dehumanized. When you disagree with ordinary people, you always get the feeling that your opinion matters to them, but with a narcissist, that is not the case. All the things about you that the narcissist claimed to like when he was charming you will somehow turn into negative attributes, and the narcissist will portray himself as a "saint" for putting up with those attributes.

He Will Hog Your Conversations

Narcissists are in love with the way people perceive them, so they will take every chance to talk about themselves. Whenever you try to have a conversation, the topic is always going to change, and it will suddenly be about them. It's never a 2-way conversation with a narcissist unless he is trying to manipulate you into thinking he cares about you. You will get to a point where you really struggle to get him to hear your views or to get him to acknowledge your feelings. When you start telling a story about something that happened to you at work, you will never get to the end of it because he is going to start his own story before you are done with yours. If you make comments on certain topics of conversation, your comments will be ignored, dismissed, or even corrected unnecessarily.

He Will Violate Your Boundaries

From very early in the relationship, the narcissist will start showing disregard for your personal boundaries. You will notice that he violates your personal space, and he has no qualms about asking you to do him favors that he has by no means earned. He will borrow your personal items or even money and fail to return it, and when you ask, he is going to say that he didn't know it was such a big deal to you — the point is to make you seem petty for insisting on boundaries that most decent people would consider reasonable.

He Will Break the Rules

The narcissist will break the rules that you set for your relationship, and other social rules, without any compunction. The problem is that sometimes, we are initially attracted to rule breakers because they seem to be "bad boys" or "rebels," but those traits are in fact tale-tell signs of narcissism. A person who breaks social norms is definitely going to break relationship rules because relationships are essentially social contracts. If someone is trying to charm you, but in your first few interactions, you observe that he cuts lines, tips poorly, disregards traffic rules, etc., you can be certain that you are dealing with a narcissist.

He Will Try to Change You

When you are in a relationship with someone, they are definitely going to change you in a few minor ways (often unintentionally). However, when you are dealing with a narcissist, he is going to make a deliberate and perceptible effort to change you, and more often than not, it won't be for the better. He will try to break you, and he will try to make you more subservient to him.

You will find yourself making concession after concession, until, in the end; any objective observer can tell you that you are under his thumb. He will cause you to lose your sense of identity so that you end up being a mere extension of him. When you get out of that relationship, you will find it difficult to figure out who you are as an individual because he would have spent the entire duration of the relationship defining and redefining you.

He Will Exhibit a Sense of Entitlement

The narcissist will demonstrate a sense of entitlement for the most part of your relationship. At first, he may seem generous and considerate just to draw you in, but after that, you will see his entitlement rear its ugly head. He will be expecting preferential treatment all the time, and he will expect you to make him a priority in your life (even ahead of your own career or your family). There will be a clear disconnect between what he offers and what he expects, and he is going to want to be the center of your universe.

He Will Try to Isolate You

Any narcissist who wants to control you and make you subservient to him understands that you have a support system of friends and family who won't stand by and let him harm you. So, one of the things he will do once he has faked affection and earned some of your trust is he is going to try and isolate you. He will insist that every time you hang out, you shouldn't bring anyone along. He will make up lies to drive a wedge between you and your friends. He will play into the conflicts that exist between you and your family members to make you lean on them a lot less. If you let him get rid of your support system, he will have free reign, and you won't stand a chance against his manipulation.

He Will Express a Lot of Negative Emotions

Narcissists trade on negative emotions because they want to be the center of attention. When you are in a relationship with one, he is going to be upset when you don't do what he wants, when you are slightly critical of him, or when you don't give him the attention he is looking for. He is going to use anger, insincere sadness, and other negative emotions to make you insecure, to get your attention, or to gain a sense of control over you. If someone you are dating throws a tantrum over minor disagreements or when you aren't able to give him attention, it means that he has a fragile ego, which is a clear sign that he could be a narcissist.

He Will Play the Blame Game

This is perhaps the most common indicator that you are in a relationship with a narcissist. He will never admit to any wrongdoing, and he will always find a way of turning everything into your fault. When anything doesn't go according to plan, he will always point out your part in it, even if he too could have done something to change the outcome of the event. He will never take responsibility for anything, and when he takes action to solve a mutual problem that you have, he will always make it clear that you owe him.

Conclusion

Thank you for making it through to the end of *Dealing with a Narcissist*, let's hope it was informative and able to provide you with all of the tools you need to retake control of your life from the narcissist that has been ruining it.

The next step is to start implementing the lessons that you have learned here in a smart and strategic way so that you can loosen the narcissist's stranglehold on your life without making yourself more of a target.

In this book, you have discovered how the mind of a narcissist works, and what makes him/her tick. When you start dealing with the narcissist in your life, you have to take these lessons to heart. You have also learned how you can identify different types of narcissists, so make sure that you figure out what kind of narcissist you are dealing with, so you can come up with the best strategy for dealing with him/her.

You have also learned how to create boundaries and stick to them when dealing with narcissists, and how to use emphatic validation when you want to criticize a narcissist. Make sure that you don't overlook this advice because it could make your life a bit easier.

You should also remember the "don'ts" that we have discussed in detail within the book. Make sure that you don't share too much information with the narcissist; you don't assume that the narcissist cares about you, you don't play the narcissist's games, you don't second guess yourself when dealing with a narcissist, and you don't assume that the narcissist's actions are personal.

There is a big difference between reading about how to deal with a person or a problem, and actually doing it in real life. When you are dealing with an actual narcissist in real life, you are going to feel scared and under pressure, and it's easy to forget the right approach when it comes to handling the situation. When you confront the narcissist, take a deep breath, and remember that you stand your best chance of getting your way when you are calm and collected.

Made in the USA
Monee, IL
06 January 2022

88044359R00046